I0449913

# Walking Through Life Paralyzed

Deinelle A. Burke

authorHOUSE®

*AuthorHouse*™
*1663 Liberty Drive*
*Bloomington, IN 47403*
*www.authorhouse.com*
*Phone: 1-800-839-8640*

© *2011 Deinelle A. Burke. All rights reserved.*

*No part of this book may be reproduced, stored in a retrieval system, or transmitted by any means without the written permission of the author.*

*First published by AuthorHouse 02/11/2011*

*ISBN: 978-1-4520-4142-1 (sc)*
*ISBN: 978-1-4520-4143-8 (e)*

*Printed in the United States of America*
*Bloomington, Indiana*

*This book is printed on acid-free paper.*

# Contents

# I Can't Give Up (Part 1)

There are moments, when I find myself wanting to just give up. But I never do. In these moments, when life is bitter, fearless and cruel, the best we can do is distorted. The messages that are arranged and presented by life are nothing but voices from a stranger telling us that we can't be and we shouldn't be who we want to be.

There are moments when it feels like nothing will go my way. Even though I can smile and show everyone that I am happy with being me, there is so much more to that. There is so much more to me that I don't even understand. I don't understand my thoughts sometimes. But I don't need to understand, and neither does the society. Instead we need to pretend we do, because the moment we understand a situation, or someone's thoughts, is the moment where we lose control of our own thoughts.

To be continued...

## Sorrow Awaits Us All

I feel a deadly sting caressing my eyes.
For so long I could barely grasp this imploding fear
And this dying life that had seem to see beyond me
I let go of my fears and fly somewhere east
To grab a bite or two
Then I see a shadow that doesn't seem to last
While this dim light is fading away.

Timeless treasures
I have failed to keep
they seem so far away now.
And I remain a prisoner of my own tears
I'm forced to watch them fall
like a raging current that kills everything
that dares to attack its waters
with unclean daggers
and fearless hooks.

# Broken Visions

I can see myself as I look out the window
An image of prosperity and laughter among the stars
With dreams suddenly faltered
A candle lit by hope and put out by desire

I can see myself as I read a romantic novel
A beautiful beginning
With such a tragic ending

I can see myself when I look at the grass
Trampled by the ones
Who don't care seem
To care for me

I can see myself as I look in the mirror
A young black boy
Who doesn't
know himself
At all

## Happy Ending

With a happy ending,
the beginning broke through.
The existence of contemporary souls,
the engine that powered our love was shattered.

A frozen, secluded and armouring life
a tempted and blithe dreamer.
The more we suffer,
the more we cry.

Countless rages.
Twenty times.
Departed hands that rape the breathing.

If you analyze their eyes,
and crystallize their mind,
you create a human undefined.
No more time to think.

Once upon a time.
We could destroy our fear.
And place small pieces,
of our imagination.

Happy endings never seemed so corrupt.

# Stage One

The beginning,
Stage one.
My surroundings are evoking; my fear is inevitable.
The questions that run through my mind are exhausting.
The time that swallows my strength is calm.
The laughter that overshadows my pain is destructive;
    instructive; productive.
Apart from the distractions and the reactions,
nothing is repressive; expressive.
It's the way we act that compensate for our friends.
The way we defeat, that prove as our revenge.
The life of a teen; the struggle.
As I look past the bars,
see myself in the mirror,
a light beams through.
A light saying it's okay; I'll find a way
Importance is key,
we all dream for significance.
It's a struggle,
but stage two can't break me down.

# Dangerous Love

*Love is a wonderful thing, but at the same time it is very powerful. You can't let it control you, because when love starts to control you, someone else gains control also. You are blinded by love that you don't see the pain they inflect on you. The moment you finally realize, it is too late.*

# If I Could Die of Happiness

We see each other
only for a moment
and then I see your heart.

Images of love
a shining star
an ever flowing river, ending upon the blissful ocean.
A blanket of joy that lifts my spirit
Condemns my soul

I'm trapped under your wing
You have me under your spell
As I fly through the mountains in the satin blue sky,
Your heart stays strong
Then you kiss me
There is nothing sweeter than the feeling of your lips

I can't say I love you
Because it is so much more than that.

I break away from this moment
and I look away
if I could die of happiness,
Bury me right next to your heart.

# *Alovera*

(Written By: Michelle Whittingham)

Such beauty;
The perfect green leaf
Internally filled with slime
A taste of bitterness

Different flavours are added
In an effort to tolerate and ingest
Yet the bitter taste lingers

Yet so nourishing and cleansing
Yet such a healing power

Everything is beautiful in some way or another.
Does this beauty belong to you or some other?
Is this the type of beauty you desire?
Does this beauty provide you with happiness?
Does this beauty embrace you?
Is this beauty warm and comforting?
Does this beauty impact your ability to love?

## Simply Love: Part One

Simply love
Contained in a capsule
Tight shut
And unbreakable
Untouched by the wind
That ragingly blows around it

Any  soul
Can hear love
Through the capsule
A strong and sincere heart, beating
It's alive
Love is alive

It watches me
As I pound on the capsule
Hoping to set it free
And feel the way lovers do

## And She Loves Me...

"I can hold her and say I love her, because I do."

Time,
is being wasted
on the truth.

Watching her,
from a distance.
Running away,
from her footsteps.

A beating heart.
But the heart is dead.
No life seen,
except the life in her eyes.

And, she loves me.

And I'm lying.
But why tell the truth,
When lies can make everyone smile?

"And, she loves me. But only in my dreams."

# A Feeling of Ignorance

She says that I'm crazy right?
She says I'm living a crazy life.
She doesn't see the hope that only makes me mad,
Or the feeling of lost promises that I wish I had.
I stopped thinking of the past
And the thoughts that just seemed to pass,
I left myself a little room to breathe.
I needed more time to see
How my mistakes really
Made the better of me.

Mistakes with you
Mistakes with me,
I wish that I could stop trusting my heart.
Maybe I should let her heart break apart.
I'd cause her smile to flip and her skin to bleed.
She'd finally be unhappy with me.

And still,
I love her so.
I can't let go.

A feeling of ignorance

I'm a victim of my own pain
My own gun that I pointed to her.
I pulled the trigger and I missed

I stay damaged like I did last fall
And I fell ten feet
But still remained six feet tall.
This is just a feeling that I feel for her
Opposite from an illusion
But opposite from the truth

A feeling of ignorance

## Simply Love: Part Two

Simply love
Escaping its capsule
Feeling the wind across its face

it was love at first sight
its smile consumes me
a smile that glistens my dull eyes
Love knows its beauty

as it smoothly flies above
Realization comes to mind
Love was made just for me

## My Love Is Gone

I stood there staring at my love for days perhaps
And there was nothing I could say
The breeze rolled over me like a blanket
Of love, and helped me catch my breath
Before I had to say goodbye.

I wish I had told her everything
before she had to drift away
before her life had given up.

I looked at her
Hugged her with all of my might
My tears rolled down her cheek
And glazed upon her red satin lips

I stroked her silky hair
Kissed her lips
But this wasn't a fairy tale.

My love was gone
and she wasn't coming back.

Goodbye.

# Simply Love: Part Three

Simply love
Moves in on me
Breaking my hidden barrier
And captures me

All at once
I am filled with love
My dry hands moisten
And my heart feels stronger

Snow falls
And I stay warm with love wrapped around me
This love
I had dreamed for

## That's When You Will Love Me

When the heavens can finally smile upon me and the
    darkness can finally fade.
I know we can find a way.
The life that I see through my blindness is bitter
the cold I feel through my sweater is moist
and someday everything will make sense.
Coarse edges upon my skin,
Fast air upon my wings.
Seven deadly sins that might someday become untainted
    with love,
not lust.
The faces we see are nothing but enemies,
peering through our wants and needs,
and one day I might be able to show them that everything
    is okay.
Nothing is wrong with being me.
Nothing is guaranteed
not even what we perceive.
Life will change;
Life will finally be our greatest dreams.
Someday,
I will be able to look at you and say I love you.
One day,
you will hold my hand and lead me to your heart.

## Simply Love: Part Four

Simply love
Had such a strong grip on my heart
Then ripped it out

Love had my heart in its hand
And squeezed it until it was crushed
Into a million pieces of nothing

Then it started to rain
I stood there
Watching love fly away

Wishing for once in my life
I never set it free

# Want Love? No Thank You.

Love;
It could've buried me alive,
So many times.
Instead it just watched me suffer
While I served its needs,
And gave it every single part of me.
I gave it my heart; soul
And everything in between,
Just to find out that it had no plans for me.
 I wasn't a slave;
Only an unwanted dream.
*Never fall in love with a fallen angel.*

Lies sound so sweet,
Because they're our unimaginable fantasies.
The truth is dull; no emotion or wit.
Yet, I rather fall in love with the truth,
Or be abstinent for love.

When you fall in love,
You lose yourself.
You blindly give all that you are
To the other person,
And in the end you're empty.

# How Long Will This Last?

Your smile is so fake. It means nothing to me.
How long will you go on pretending?
I'm tempted to ask, and it's perfectly clear.
Your feelings for me are ending.

Flashing lights that appear,
when you look me straight in the eye.
Your hugs so awkward and obscene
Used to soar me through the sky.

Forcing a laugh, when nothing was said,
to act as if you care.
How long will it last,
till you finally admit you've moved on from the love we once
    shared?

# Unnoticeable

She has the prettiest smile,
but she's not smiling at me.
She's smiling at the person she wants me to be.
I am unnoticeable.

# Children Are the Future

*Even though we are all different in many ways, just like the flowers, weeds, and poppies, everyone should be treated equal. Even though it does not always happen, the world is definitely going to change. Children are the first step, because when these young children change their ways at a young age, they will grow up and carry it with them forever, hopefully creating an influence in the world.*

# Alice

She dreamed only of a world,
Where her imagination would come to life
The impractical was surely feasible in a land of her own
Singing flowers and talking rabbits,
So fallacious but beautiful
In this land so flaunting
The truth starts to surface
Yet no truth can exist in a world so fake
A world held only by a figment of her imagination
Her reality was hidden all along by a dream
She dreamed only of a world...
She longed only for a wonderland where dreams came true.

## When You Wish Upon a Star

I wished upon a star
then my sister got shot,
and for some reason I thought I knew why.
Because I hated her guts
and couldn't stand the way she always made me cry.
She was the oldest, smartest
and the favourite of us all,
then when my parents came around I was a dead wall.
"Dead" sounded well,
and quite fine with her name.
"Jane Adams is dead!"
And this time it wasn't a game.

Now she's dead and life is too,
because I thought things would change.
But now my parents don't talk as much,
since the day she went away.

I wanted her room,
because it was big and tall,
but to "cherish" her,
my parents said not to touch it at all.

Life was not what I expected;
sadly I wished she was alive.
I missed how I couldn't stand her
and how she always made me cry.
Now I'm sorry,
but she's never coming back,
no matter what I do.
But it was my mom who said when you wish upon a star
anything can come true.

# The Hardest Part

Warm wind rushed by
Goodbye was the easiest part.
Waiting for a long time
for the pressure on my skin to stop
the smile to force its way out,
But my heart was frozen for the ones I pitied.
I was going back to Canada.
Where the birds left us in the winter to stay warm,
where my smile
would finally be happy.

In the air
I felt like a bird
my spirit still wasn't free.
Crying was the easiest part,
thinking about my mother.
Would she remember my appearance?
Was she still the same mother I knew?
I laid my head back,
closed my eyes.
I didn't want to fly anymore.

I ran towards my mother
her smile as soft as my cotton sweater.
I hugged her because I loved her.
She knew.
She knew I didn't want to go back
by the scars on my back,
And on my heart.
But I had to.

Five years later,
Only 11.
Saying goodbye was the hardest part.
But I had to.

I was leaving to go somewhere warm
like the birds.
But was it safe?
The pressure on my skin
was a sign of hate
they hated me.
Why was I going back?

# A Dream

I blasted to the moon
then did a back flip in space
and it felt like I could fly.

I suddenly appeared on a cloud
so soft and round
then fell through
and soared in the sky.

I fought off a snake
with an old garden rake
as it chased me around the bay.

Just as he came close
a dragon appeared
and scared that mean snake away.

I jumped on the dragon
and flew high in the air
then blasted down to the sea.

I floated to the top
and closed my eyes
then woke up from a wonderful dream.

I went to the kitchen
for a glass of milk
Then I went back to sleep.

And before you know it
I swam right to the bottom
with my dragon in the deep blue sea.

# Daddy's Little Girl

A little girl with a big heart
and a big smile.
So innocent.

Daddy looks at his beautiful blessing.
The amazing wonder that was sent to him from heaven.

Her eyes are big and brown.
Her lips are soft as she kisses his cheek.
Her nose looks like his.

He is compelled to hold her
and promise never to let go.
If he lets go, he worries that she might never be the same.

As she grows older
He face is changed.
Her attitude is matured.

Still,
her eyes are brown as she looks upon her aging father.
Her lips still soft and glazed with red lipstick.
Her nose still looks like his.

Daddy's little girl she will forever be.

# Doves

Seventeen doves grabbed a boy in his sleep.
His hair is ripped off
by their soft white feet.
Their wings flapped as the sun
glistened in their eyes.

Their eyes seek disaster.

But they are so beautiful.

These beauties of white start to yell:
"Hell is only minutes away."

I am being brought up to the skies of the unknown.
Then I see a boy, falling past me.

## I Know Your Hands So Well

I wish I could go back in time,
before you got so angry.
Back to the only time you said you loved me.

After a while, I began to know your hands so well.
They were always there in the worst ways.
And they always aimed for my face.

It's only a miracle that people can look at me and smile.
I smile back.
I used to look at them and know what they were thinking.
They thought I was happy.
But inside...

I didn't have an inside.
It was always outside...
It was what was happening outside.
My fears were outside.
My tears were outside.

And even though you stopped, the pain won't go away.
If you had let me speak back then,
I would look you in the eye and say:
"You should never have abused my daddy. You should have
    loved me like you said you did."
But there was only so much I could do.

# Respect

*It is very easy to get in a "friendship" with people who are going to use you and take advantage of you. At the same time, friendship can carry you far. Over the past eighteen years of my life, I have realized that respect does not come easily. It takes time to form and it takes time to give. The world has to realize that life is too short for bad attitudes towards people we care about or not. We should treat everyone with respect because the one person we treat wrong is the same person who we need to teach us an inspiring life lesson. There are going to be many people we don't like, but we need to think about why we don't like them. Sometimes the reasons are justifiable. Most of the time, we say we don't like someone because of how they dress, how they act, how they talk. Those reasons are not justifiable at all. Also, saying you don't like someone, does not mean you cannot show respect. I wrote poems about respect to describe how foolish we, as a society, behave to one another. A better world, a better society starts with one person. Respect is the first step.*

# When It's All Said and Done

At times
you cause my own world to deceive me
you control my actions
and speak my mind.

Immortal you seem to be only in my eyes

The constant pain from you're harsh words
The devilish smile that only you could pull off
You're ears so large
They make me wonder if you can hear my thoughts of you.

Instantly
My thoughts seem to pause
And I'm frozen
And worried you're going to hurt me again
Like you always do

Yet
When it's all said and done
You're the only one who can really make the pain go away.

..

Maybe that's why I'm so mad.

## Boomerang

When you let it go,
you are letting go of the responsibilities that were set to
you.
You lose all the respect you once gained,
and you destroy the love that was once in you're dying
heart.
You stand there with nothing else to do.
Your hurtful words and actions fly through the air,
and the wind looks at them in disgust and fear.
Don't turn your back.
Don't try to forget.
Because pretty soon the boomerang will come right back to
you.
What goes around comes around.

## For My Mother

You're the true definition of love.
You're my heart and soul,
my light and darkness,
my happy and sad.
You're everything to me.

Life is just a big blanket of nothing,
until you hug me or tell me you love me.

I'm only strong because you made me strong.
I can only stand tall, because I am able to lean on your
      shoulder.

And mother,
when heaven is ready for its new queen,
just bring me with you,
so I can be happy forever.

# This and Life

I'm sorry darling,
but I know you can't forgive me.

Life can end any moment,
but try and enjoy the ride.
Because I'm only human,
and I can't make you happy.
You're more than perfect.
So, speak my name.
No. You can't because life is pulling you back.
Utter it slowly, and then I'll wipe away your tears.
I don't want you to cry.
I'll die for you if you want me to.

This is it.
This is where you say you love me,
and you'll always be there.

Close your eyes,
and don't cry if I hold you,
because I want you to be happy.

This is the moment,
where you thank me for making you happy,
where you finally give me another chance.

But this is a dream.
Unfortunately, life is a reality.

# Bright Lights

(Written By: Michelle Whittingham)

One can see the signs;
turns the eyes
dismiss and cover
the truth.

When will you notice this pain?
When will you end it?

My eyes are uncovered
the lights are on so bright
It will turn the night into day.

This energy won't last forever.
It's fading away...

Until it's gone.

# Life Lessons

The clock will keep ticking,
because time waits for no man.

Importance, you may gain,
but you shall never be respected.

You will always live your life
being scared, alone and depressed.
You're afraid of me because I am never around.
Oddly enough, you love me when I say I hate you.

Does that make sense?
Tell me the truth, does that make sense?

Life will never make sense.
Life doesn't always have a point.
Some can look at life and say it has no importance.
So I look at you,
and ask you,
Honestly,
Why should you be important in unimportance?
Is it because you want to stand out?

You will never stand out.
You are weak.
You will always be afraid of me.

So take my hand,
and don't let go.

You need to trust me
Even though you are afraid of me.
Because if you let go of my hand,
this stupidity called "life"
Will come back around and get rid of you.

We can't control life like we used to anymore.
Why?
Because the moment you start to control life,
Is the same moment someone starts controlling you.
Control is an evil thing.

You will never gain importance that way.

# The Road Unknown

*The road unknown is scary, but it is always worth the prize and the goal you set for yourselves. More than anything, getting there is the hardest part, because it hurts, people are going to give up on you, and sooner or later you are going to be the only one walking that dark and scary road. Without faith, determination, and ambition you will never succeed in this cruel world. Just believe in yourself that you can make it, and you can make a change in yourself and the others around you who love you or hate you.*

# Ten City Lights

Ten city lights lined up on Tipsy Street.
The city is dark,
yet lights shines through.

The night is cold,
the mood is smooth.
The roads are used by only a few drunks.
They can't see the road even though the city lights lead
    their way.
They swerve and spin.
The city lights watch over,
and flicker in disappointment.
All of a sudden,

Crash.

Nine city lights lined up on Tipsy Street.
The street gets darker and darker each night.

# Untainted Eyes

Pretty little girl.
Beautiful eyes.
When she cries her tears wash her troubles away.
Then she transforms.

Because of carefree words,
The harsh frustration stays bottled inside
As she tries to think of reasons
Not to care.

The fiction is her reality.
The lies are her truths.

Only one way to stop her damnation.
By covering her sorrow.
Her blackened mind tells her
That she isn't beautiful,
While her heart is hardly being heard.

Her makeup is deadly.
It changes her into a dark woman.
A true reflection of how she feels.

She's empty.
She's fake.

Then she cries...

The demon is slowly crawling down her cheeks.
She looks in the mirror and doesn't recognize
The beautiful eyes that were once untainted.

# I Kind of Hurt My Best Friend

I ask her to stop her tears. This lazy river we are drowning
    in
fills me with sadness. I silently step into a
fragment of time where smiles were
often and fear was
never
seen.

She had eyes that could see through me.
"But, I never knew her at all."

I threw her dreams away,
only yesterday.

I made her cry,
and I smiled.

I distanced myself,
from her.

I killed her.

She was my best friend,
and I let her die.

My weak faith in her
was the only thing
that kept her alive.

# The Great Escape

Smile.
Journey to the mountains of Tibet;
Remember the anxiety you once implicated within your
    life.
The frosty, icy platforms
Stride the valley of Yosemite;
Observe the way you can at last smile.
The dampness soaks your feet, the water smooth and cool.
Flatten the sands of Egypt;
Understand why you made it this far.
The sand upon your skin, the heat glazing upon your
    forehead.
It's all existent.
Don't be frightened to let go of the tough times.
Flee from the fear and the stress that proclaims you.
Break away from the malevolence that once conceited your
    mind.
The Great Escape starts with a smile.

# Mama's Hands

"My hands will protect you, my child."

That's all Mama said.
But Mama's hands are in a scary place.
All they do is wipe the tears
from her eyes.

She lies in hell, suffering
bruises and threats.
Her hands can't protect, but she stays
strong.

I hug her, and I say it's alright mother.

"It's time for my hands to protect you."

# Walk On Water

Ambitious yet afraid,
the soul is a sign.
It's telling my mind to cry when it wants to.
The loss of our heart is gained by the depths of our beliefs.

Anything is possible.
I could walk on water,
only if you held my hand along the way.

I rather sail a boat.
Even though boats are tainted with the water I fear.
I can't give up.
The tides are high and crystal blue.
And the only one stopping me here is you.

You're telling me to wait before I do something stupid.
But nothing is stupider than the concept of life and death;
it is something we don't have control over.

Should I establish such a state of mind
that might cover my weakness?
I could walk on water if I was a little stronger.
Yet, strength wasn't one of my strong points.

# Memories

I couldn't sense her.
Her skin was as pale
 as the life I'd been living.
Her eyes were cold,
as they sent shivers down my spine.

It was a winter night,
but my body was hot.
Sweating in all my shame
and indignity,
I whispered her name.
No call out for help,
because it was over.
No finishing screams,
 because I ended it.

I ended her life
and all the dreams she kept with her.
I kissed her softly,
and then walked away
with the last piece of the puzzle.
My memories.

As I wandered down the street,
many things were going through my mind.
The cars passing
were merely a gradual distraction,
at an attempt to make me forget
what happened.
The street lights
were a replica of the knife's stem

and shimmering sharp point.
My heart was oil on water,
separated from my body.
It felt like someone was beating the heart inside this cold
    empty shell,
making these decisions for me.

In this world,
there is always someone to talk to,
look up to...

But I don't
live in this world,
I live in
my own.
In my world,
no one is there;
nobody cares
if you are
scared of
life itself.
You are just
a feather
on an eagle,
similar to
them all.
No one
is different.
Everyone thinks
the same thoughts
or wants
the same things.
Hearts beat
at the

same pace,
except
for the one
who doesn't
think like the rest.
Me.

You could say I'm young,
but I've been through the worst.
I don't want the same thing they want.
The heart inside of this shell doesn't beat the same way
    theirs does.

I'm sorry I stopped hers from beating,
but it was the only way I could get what I wanted.

## The Snow Will Always Fall

Ice and frostbite in my life.
Fear that plunges into the depths of reality.
Harsh but sensitive understanding.

A discrete understanding of what lies beneath this cold and
    raging snow.
Heat from all hands to melt this, once soft and calm life;
to finally achieve what was missing from our hearts.

And as I mix both fiery heat which is the love I share with
    the world;
With this dreadful and spiteful cold
Which fills souls every day,
Causing pain to those around,
I soon forget it all.

I watch the snow melt away.

Sadly, only for the season.

# A Letter to You

Dear best friend,

I imagine you're smiling,
or even laughing right now,
because you always did everything I couldn't.
Even though you're watching me from up above
I know you're happier up there,
than when you were down here.

Nothing happens down here anymore.
The place is silent and boring.
But then, I just pop in one of our funny home videos we
    made together.
Then I want to smile.
And even though I'm going to miss you, its okay,
because my heart doesn't cry anymore.

Want to know a secret?
Sometimes, when I close my eyes,
then open them and I would see you right in front of me.
I would talk to you, and laugh and smile...

Then when I blinked,
you would be gone.

Then all the laughter went away.

But the truth is,
As long as you're laughing,
I will always be happy.
You were always doing the things I couldn't.
You will never be forgotten.

From your best friend.

# Hold On

Holding onto a dream won't carry you far
Let it go
They say dreams never come true

Holding onto forever will only last for a moment
Move on from the promises you keep with yourself
Forever is just a word

Holding onto the truth will never be real
Truth is only the fear
Of what might become of us in the future

Keep holding on
The truth is: Dreams that last forever are worth holding
    onto.

## My Life

I know that God exists
in the life of mine.

My life where everything goes wrong.
The smile I force
is only temporary
until I fall again.

My young bones will
break after the
first mile I run,
at an attempt to discover
what my life has become.

My eyes will tear
and my neck will snap
then silently try to
fix back!
Fight back!

Come back to life.

I know that God exists
in this life of mine

my life where
everything goes
wrong.

## Walking Through Life Paralyzed

Walking through life paralyzed.
Burdens so heavy put upon my back.
Lights too bright flashing in my eyes.
People I used to call "friends",
Kick my knees while I'm down.
I need help to lift up this weight holding me down.
I can't move my neck.
I don't want to turn my neck, to see the dangers that lie
    ahead of me.

Suddenly, someone grabs my hand,
and my burdens are gone.
My eyes regain focus and my friends help me on my
    journey.
My weight is the last thing on my mind,
as I leave it in the dirt behind me.
The dangers, I can now face.

I was paralyzed, but only temporarily.
I am stronger now.

# What Happens Next?

To me, the world is immoral. The world in unsafe, unjust, and unfair. Society is corrupt, and depraved. So what? The question is what do we do now? Once we have absorbed this truth what happens next? The world is cruel and we all realize that once again. Once again we are being told the exact same thing for the many years humans have existed. Does something need to happen next? The question is, "should their even be a change?" If we wanted to make a change, we would have made a change. I, wanting to make a change, start with myself. I change my perception on life and myself every day. Therefore keeping myself positive and grounding my responsibility to be a better role model. Change starts with one person, and not everyone is like me, so all I can do is hope. All I can do is remind them how cruel the world is, hoping one day someone else can try and make a change with themselves.

# Martin Luther King

When someone can look at me,
and tell me that I have inspired them,
I can only smile and think of you.
I thank them and shake their hand.

When someone can look at me in disgust,
And hate me, for who I am,
Call me inappropriate names, and swear that I won't make
    it somewhere
I can only smile, and think of you
But what is the society, you worked so hard to create,
    coming to?

We are all equals.
And whether we all know it or not, that's how it shall
    stand.
Nothing is scarier than the life some people live.
Nothing is more heartbreaking than the loss of one you
    love,
Caused by an undignified battle of race.
And still, I fail to understand how your teachings
and justified actions could have gone in vein.

I will never forget your words.
And though I was not there August 28th 1963,
"I Have a Dream" will forever live on.
A dream about hope,
and what we wish of this world.
A dream that help us all to see,
that equality is only around the corner,
for the ones who have yet to attain it.

Now is the time.
Now is the time for us to start believing that a change will
    come.
Without hope, there is nothing.
We need to try and understand each other.
Justice will soon be a reality.

Yes, we are Negroes.
But, only we know what that name means.
It means we are powerful.
We have the power to make a change in ourselves,
and the world around us.
We can do it all.
There is nothing holding us back,
because we have been through the pain.

Martin Luther King,
You came to teach us all a lesson,
whether we are black or white.
I learned it,
but there are many people who haven't.
There are many people who are drowning us in their
    prejudice.
I am strong enough to help them.
I am strong enough to help them change.

One day,
our world will be just like your dream.

# Society in My Backyard

Unethical thinking,
loud depression.
Solemn understanding and twisted fate.
The keys that create a misty soul.

Paralyzed and tampered with;
Colourful and so few.
The political fools;
Fools on their own behalf.

A supreme effort of injustice
and the victory of destruction
outside a poor man's house.

The fear that wanders the dead, black allies.
The eyes that gaze through our windows.
Typical; physical; perceivable.

Not considerable; understandable.
It's the society we live in.
The society that doesn't really know what to do anymore.

# Upon The Darkness

Mortality feels only seconds away
It feels closed and fractured
Upon my flared eyes
Come still; and wonder softly
Dream of a tainted shadow
That light can pierce through
It can feel darkness

Darkness can lie in its shell
And rest peacefully

Mortality happens twice
Three times when eyes are shut

Friendly ghost
Come and feel the wrath I show
Open your eyes
Let your darkness glow.

# The Science of Fear

Fear.
Compels the vociferous to silence,
for pride is no longer superior
when it arrives.


The mentality reacts,
it gives us haunting signals.
It damages us.

Our safe becomes the dangerous;
our light becomes our darkness.
Fear.
It condemns us and traps us under its wing.
We can't move.
We stand there frozen like the great oceans in winter.

Fear.
We shiver at the name.
We are fearful of humanity and the consequences of our
    actions.
Can a poet scientifically study fear through the
    combination of thoughts and words?

Fear.
It is given only to those who seek it.

# Your Powerful Words

Lord, you are my Sheppard.
Your kingdom is my home.
I await your glory
for your name is my shield.
I've used you many times,
in times where I could have fended for myself.
I've played with your love.

And this time...
I'm at your feet
I raise my head,
and I ask you why.

Why is the world such a scary place?
Why do I look this way?
Why does life seem to just let people go?
Why my lord, do you love me so?

As the tears roll down my face
I can feel you wiping them away.
I'll listen to your powerful words,
and I'll finally be strong.

## Windows and Doors

I'm trapped in a box with windows and doors.
They hold my secrets,
and heard my stories.

When I look outside,
I don't see reality.
The reality is inside this box.

The windows allow me to
see the fake world around me.
The doors allow me to walk in it.

And I'm scared to;
because all I know is
the reality I live in.

That only the windows and doors can see.

# What the World Has Become

We are broken
but we are fixed

fighting the ones we love
Hearts filled with rage
Cries aren't heard
Overshadowed with violence

Speak all at once
Say something meaningful and true.
Make your words swallow me
In delight and love
Or just destroy me as you feel necessary
Drown me in your hate
And discrimination

I feel the wind with no air
I see the ocean with no water
Then I realize that this is what the world has become

You won't remember me when I'm alone
We are broken, not fixed

# My World of Blue

In my world of blue
The sun can't shine
I'm dark, scared and hungry

But,
Life always has it's reasons
Even though they may be unclear

In my world of blue
I look up and see their pretty faces glaring at me
I look down, and see their pretty shoes almost stepping on me

But,
Darkness will always fade away
The light will soon shine through

In my world of blue
I lay my head behind this restaurant, and close my eyes
The sounds that wake me up while I sleep on the hard,
     dirty floor
Are the sounds coming from my stomach

But,
The worst starvation can do is kill me

So in my world of blue
I need to stand tall
Because it's time to let the yellow shine through.

Nothing will change
until I change it.

# Complicated

staring at the TV
when the powers out
and the lights are off
with the door closed --

makes you
think about things
that you never
thought you
cared for

I feel myself
crawling on the wall
then falling
out the window

at times
I wish my life
made sense

I look in
the broken mirror
and my
skin is dry
with the cold air
damply moistening it
with fear

my feet
can't hold this
pressure
for much longer

my face is
flawless but
my mind is twisted

why do I sit
at a TV with
no power

I'm expecting
someone

maybe a friend
to sit here
with me

--

# Drunken Hearts

Drunken hearts
end in sorry tears.
Collapsed visions
of what we wish
existed.

# The Play, The Murder
# and The Soul

# The Play Called Life

Do you ever feel like you were disconnected from everyone else who existed in the world? Worse yet, everyone who *seemed* to exist? It is a state of mind. A space of time where everybody was frozen and I was the odd one out; the black sheep who baaed at the sight of the swift yet steady air. Air that purposely made me wonder – about nothing at all.

Apart from *this and that*, I can barely remember my name. All I recall is the sudden urge I have to sleep past midnight and eat only before noon. My fragile connection to *whatever* is non-existent, merely because I serve no importance. Suppose, even for a moment that anything that is irrelevant, does not exist. *You don't know me; you're not a friend of mine.* What importance could I possibly serve? *Keys to Success?* Was that my importance? To shovel the dirt off my eyes and see a destiny that was never mine? Was this life a possession? Was it something that I controlled, and took pride in? This wasn't my life. It was the memory of an old faith, that I dropped somewhere on the road to freedom. I'm only life's puppet.

And then by chance, I happen to look behind me, while on the road to freedom, and see the fear that once engulfed me. I see the solemn emptiness that is somehow attracted to my brightened soul. I am carried away by forgotten truths and misleading assumptions. They make me what I am today. Life depends on us humans, because music is nothing without its orchestra. Life needs slaves. *Without the ones to feel pain, how can pain exist?* And that's all that matters now.

I must admit that I regret some decisions that I made in the past. After my heart was savagely beaten and served on a golden platter to my enemies, I lost respect for the ones who cared about me. I felt all of my strength disappear and trap itself in a glass jar. Away from me. Far away from me.

I stand there, empty. With nothing to live for, except my mother, and perhaps one more, I stretch my bones across a new born baby and wipe its tears away. The baby is nothing more than a sponge that hasn't grasped reality by the hands... yet. Still there is nothing left to wish for. Nothing to dream for. Life has already surrendered me to its dreadful fate. What is a dream? Only a dying hope. *The moment we are born, is the moment we begin to die.*

Almost at the end, I can take a step back from this *thing* I've lived, and I can smile at all my certain accomplishments. I might cry here and there, but I'll smile for the most part. I might sigh heavily at the over load of troubles I've caused, and dangers I've wished upon others. Their insincere forgiveness has only made me weaker.

I always feel like I am disconnected from everyone else who exists in the world. Or *seems* to exist. I'm just an actor in their play called *Life*. They all take advantage of me, some more than others. Most of these humans don't speak to me. But they all know me. Now, I'm not suggesting that the world revolves around me. But, in this dream – this dying hope to finally exist – it does.

# Bobby

Her name was Bobby. Her hair was new born. Her hazel eyes twinkled in the bright ceiling lamp that hanged ten feet above us. Her nose was not like mine. Why would it be? Her lips were thin. So thin, that I could barely see them at all. Only five days old, I watched this baby, who was going to become a woman so quickly. My woman. The woman I could hurt and abuse. The woman I could laugh with and tickle.

From morning until night, she haunted me at only five months old. Constant cries from her, as if she hated me. I could not keep running back and forth. I wasn't her friend, or anyone who cared. The hands that touched her were not comforting and calm. If I hurt her, The Law wouldn't even arrest me. My life would quickly become a closed book. Fate was already decided. No need for another climax. That baby wouldn't want me to come upstairs. I prayed for her to stop crying, and she did. Life was too short for foolish games.

The days went by. I began to enjoy her presence. She was only five years old. She loved to dance, and swore she would become a dancer. She was a smart little girl. She has just begun elementary school. I had only begun calling her by her name.

*My last one was Bobby. A charming and sophisticated young boy he became. Bobby knew my name and he would say it when we went out for walks in the park. He was strong, and spoke his mind. I remember once:*

*Bobby was only thirteen. I think that he was upset from the night before, and decided not to say good morning. So I hit him in his face. Then I kicked him as far as my leg could reach. He told me that he hated me, and then he ran off. At first, I could care less, but I began to feel bad. I realized that I would regret my actions, soon.*

*I thought that he had forgiven me, but maybe not. At nineteen, he decided he didn't need me anymore, and enlisted into the army. Such sorrow I felt. I thought to myself, maybe it was because of what had happened six years ago. Was I to be blamed?*

*"Why?"*

*"Why what?"*

*"What have I done to you? Why are you leaving?"*

*"I wish I could tell you. Some things are better left unsaid you told me once. Once you tell me who you really are, I will tell you why I have finally decided to leave. I will write you though. Goodbye."*

*And he wrote. He wrote many times.*

I called her Bobby, at an attempt to relive my past and fix it. She was Bobby, my friend who left me. She took his place instantly. I gave her an identity. I created her.

*I got a package from the Canadian Forces one day. They sent me a letter stating that Bobby was dead. There were some photos of him and the "guys", hanging out in the trenches. He was smiling. Never saw that smile since we used to go for outings in the park. There were pictures of him in battle. He once told me that he would never hold my gun. It was too heavy. He was scared of guns. It was all lies. There was one picture. Of dead bodies lying in the dusty road. A black arrow is pointing to one of the dead bodies. I guessed that was Bobby. I didn't cry once, but I was sad. It was the most pain I felt in years. I hated him for leaving me, twice. I took the photo, and I put in on the wall.*

At fifteen, she started high school. She wasn't like the other girls, talkative and preppy. I made her like that. She had to be like *Bobby. And he was never the talkative type.* She did well in school, and soon later applied for the School of Arts. When I received her acceptance letter, I tore it up. I couldn't let her leave. She was mine. I didn't want a repeat of the last incident. All her friends were accepted into university, and she was sad that she didn't. But I could care less.

At age 19, she came in the living room. I took out the gun that *Bobby* said was scary, and I shot her.

I dragged her outside, threw her on the dusty road, and wiped away the blood that was seeping from the hole in her head. I fixed her hair, extended one leg, flexed the other; pointed the foot towards the knee, lay her arm over her head. It was a lovely sight. Then I took a picture and walked away.

*I look at the war photo. There is a black arrow pointing to a girl, named Bobby. A beautiful girl, who became a woman so quickly.*

# My Soul's Disposition

The troubled mind fights for peace, in times of solemn and swift defeat. The majority of this life I live is almost over. My mind has almost cried without the distinct limitation of these wings that struggle to carry me above the clouds. And almost without realizing it, I notice myself, this black and bruised heart, felt and attacked with a saddened sword and a depressed arrow.

Too many plays my heart has acted. Too many smiles I have been forced to show. Not enough tears have flown from my eyes; I am not a man. Yet, even grown men can cry. So why do I hide my souls disposition? Who am I acting for? A judge? Probably, but only God can judge me. Maybe a king and queen? Perhaps, but I do not believe in any other royalty.

Life means no more than what it means. My life meant something more, long ago. In the time when heroes were praised and villains were feared. Now my eyes are at the back of my head and I see the moon where the sun should be. Life doesn't make sense anymore. That's where my story starts.

Want someone to love you? Just break their heart. I love. I loved. And still I run for more heart break, though it's unknown. What for? So she can notice me perhaps. So she can acknowledge my soul's disposition.

The battle has already been won. I was defeated. The hope of victory was lost in the waves, after I jumped off the ship. Only cowards jump ship because they are not brave enough to race the crumbling under their feet. I have no importance. I have no name. Think of me as a troubled mind. I'll think of you as someone who pretended to care about my story.

www.ingramcontent.com/pod-product-compliance
Lightning Source LLC
Chambersburg PA
CBHW020335290526
45785CB00005B/2026